VIETNAM

By Jennifer Lombardo
and Kaitlyn Duling

EXPLORING WORLD CULTURES

Cavendish Square

Published in 2025 by Cavendish Square Publishing, LLC
2544 Clinton Street, Buffalo, NY 14224

Second Edition

Library of Congress Cataloging-in-Publication Data

Names: Lombardo, Jennifer, author. | Duling, Kaitlyn, author.
Title: Vietnam / Jennifer Lombardo and Kaitlyn Duling.
Description: Second edition. | Buffalo, NY : Cavendish Square Publishing, [2025] | Series: Exploring world cultures | Includes bibliographical references and index.
Identifiers: LCCN 2024031518 | ISBN 9781502672889 (library binding) | ISBN 9781502672872 (paperback) | ISBN 9781502672896 (ebook)
Subjects: LCSH: Vietnam--Juvenile literature.
Classification: LCC DS556.3 .L66 2025 | DDC 959.7--dc23/eng/20240807
LC record available at https://lccn.loc.gov/2024031518

Writers: Kaitlyn Duling; Jennifer Lombardo (second edition)
Editor: Jennifer Lombardo
Copyeditors: Jill Keppeler and Danielle Haynes
Designer: Deanna Lepovich

The photographs in this book are used by permission and through the courtesy of: Cover November27/Shutterstock.com; pp. 4, 12 Guitar photographer/Shutterstock.com; p. 5 Hien Phung Thu/Shutterstock.com; p. 6 kid315/Shutterstock.com; p. 7 Daengpanya Atakorn/Shutterstock.com; p. 8 hecke61/Shutterstock.com; p. 9 darkpurplebear/Shutterstock.com; p. 10 Vitalii Karas/Shutterstock.com; p. 11 satoriphoto/Shutterstock.com; p. 13 Pawel Michalowski/Shutterstock.com; p. 14 Nguyen Quang Ngoc Tonkin/Shutterstock.com; p. 15 Ho VanTri/Shutterstock.com; p. 16 Dong Nhat Huy/Shutterstock.com; p. 17 MinhducMorri/Shutterstock.com; p. 18 Huy Thoai/Shutterstock.com; p. 19 Dragon Images/Shutterstock.com; p. 20 Duong Hoang Dinh/Shutterstock.com; p. 21 Mark Green/Shutterstock.com; p. 22 Nature-Andy/Shutterstock.com; p. 23 al clark/Shutterstock.com; p. 24 NguyenQuocThang/Shutterstock.com; p. 25 xuanhuongho/Shutterstock.com; p. 26 Maria Wold/Shutterstock.com; p. 27 LouisNguyen/Shutterstock.com; p. 28 Matthew Nichols1/Shutterstock.com; p. 29 Chzu/Shutterstock.com.

CPSIA compliance information: Batch #CW25CSQ: For further information contact Cavendish Square Publishing LLC at 1-877-980-4450.

Printed in the United States of America

CONTENTS

Introduction 4

Chapter 1 Geography 6

Chapter 2 History 8

Chapter 3 Government 10

Chapter 4 The Economy 12

Chapter 5 The Environment 14

Chapter 6 The People Today 16

Chapter 7 Lifestyle 18

Chapter 8 Religion 20

Chapter 9 Language 22

Chapter 10 Arts and Festivals 24

Chapter 11 Fun and Play..........................26

Chapter 12 Food 28

Glossary...30

Find Out More 31

Index..32

INTRODUCTION

Vietnam is a long, skinny country in Southeast Asia. It has several large cities. It also has mountains and tropical forests. In the northern part of the country, the **climate** tends to be cool and dry. Farther south, it gets warmer and wetter.

In northern Vietnam, farmers grow rice on raised steps called terraces.

Vietnam has a long and interesting history. Humans have lived there for hundreds of thousands of years. The country was controlled for parts of its history by the Chinese and French. After two wars, it finally became fully independent in the 1970s.

People who live in Vietnamese cities live much like people in other cities. In the countryside, most people are farmers. However, no matter where they live, the Vietnamese are generally very proud of their country.

In the city of Hoi An in central Vietnam, people mainly get around either on foot or by bike or boat.

GEOGRAPHY

Although Vietnam is one country, it has three separate geographic **regions**. In the north, there are rice terraces and the Red River **Delta**. The regular flooding that happens in the delta makes this land very fertile, or good for farming. Hanoi, Vietnam's capital, is the north's major city.

FACT!
Most of Vietnam's smaller, or minority, **ethnic** groups live in the Truong Son Mountains.

Son Doong Cave in central Vietnam is one of the largest caves in the world.

In the middle, there are flat stretches of land near the coast. The middle region also has the longest mountain range in Vietnam: the Truong Son Mountains. The southern region has the Mekong River Delta as well as Vietnam's largest city, Ho Chi Minh City.

THE RAINY SEASON

In southern Vietnam, it's warm year round. There are two seasons: dry and wet. In central Vietnam, people who live on the coastal plains are in danger from tropical storms called typhoons. The typhoon season falls between July and November.

The Mekong River runs through south Vietnam. It is long and splits off into nine smaller rivers, so it is often called the River of Nine Dragons.

HISTORY

The Vietnamese people have often had to fight for their freedom. For many hundreds of years, Vietnam was under Chinese control. The people fought the Chinese several times. Finally, in 1428, they overthrew the Chinese for good.

*During Vietnam's fight for independence, **resistance** fighters called Viet Cong used tunnels to get around without letting enemy soldiers see them. Today, people can visit and walk through some of the tunnels.*

FACT!

Before the Chinese first took over in 111 BCE, Vietnam was split into several different kingdoms.

When Ho Chi Minh died, he was laid to rest in this large building in Hanoi. Vietnamese people as well as tourists, or visitors from other countries, come here to honor his memory.

In the mid-1800s, France took control. They treated the Vietnamese poorly. In 1945, Vietnamese **Communists** took control of northern Vietnam. France kept control of the South. For decades, the two sides fought. China supported the North. The United States supported the South. In 1975, the North won. The two halves were reunited under a Communist government a year later.

UNCLE HO

Ho Chi Minh, who was nicknamed "Uncle Ho" by the Vietnamese, led the resistance to French rule. He started a secret Communist group called the Viet Minh. In September 1945, Ho Chi Minh announced that Vietnam was an independent country, ruled by the Viet Minh.

GOVERNMENT

Vietnam is still a Communist country today. This means that most things, including businesses, are controlled by the government. Vietnam has its own **constitution**. It has three branches, or parts, of its government: legislative, executive, and judicial.

In this picture, both the Communist flag (left) and Vietnamese flag (right) are flying.

Vietnam holds elections to choose members of the National Assembly. This is the legislative branch, or the one that makes the laws. The executive branch enforces the laws, or makes sure people follow them. In Vietnam, this includes the prime minister and their **cabinet**. The judicial branch is made up of the courts. It makes sure the laws are made and enforced fairly.

FACT!
As of 2024, the president of Vietnam is a man named Tô Lâm. The prime minister is named Phạm Minh Chính.

The Vietnamese government meets in Hanoi.

TWO LEADERS

Vietnam has a president as well as a prime minister. The president appoints, or chooses, certain important government leaders—including the prime minister. They are also the face of Vietnam inside and outside the country.

THE ECONOMY

For most of its history, Vietnam has been a country that is supported by farming. Rice, coffee, and rubber are all produced in the country and sold around the world. Vietnam's major trading partners are the United States and China. However, it trades with other countries as well.

Vietnam makes and sells a lot of ***incense****. This woman is gathering up dried incense bundles.*

DOI MOI

After independence, Vietnam's **economy** was very poor. In 1986, the government put a system called Doi Moi in place. This system allowed the Vietnamese to own their own businesses. Doi Moi helped the Vietnamese economy get stronger over time.

During the COVID-19 **pandemic**, nearly every country had economic problems. However, Vietnam bounced back much faster than most other countries. This caused big companies such as Dell and Apple to open businesses there. Since then, the country's biggest exports, or goods it sells to other countries, have been computers and cell phones.

FACT!

Tourism is a big part of Vietnam's economy. Many Vietnamese work as tour guides or in hotels.

In the city of Hoi An, the economy is mainly supported by made-to-order clothing shops. Visitors can choose the fabric and the style of their clothing, and workers will make the clothes in just a few days.

THE ENVIRONMENT

Like other parts of the world, Vietnam is facing problems with its environment, or natural world. Waste from factories pollutes, or dirties, the air and water. Vietnam has some of the worst air quality in the world. Many people wear masks to guard against the smoke and dust in the air. Vietnam is also one of the five countries with the worst plastic pollution in its waterways and on its beaches.

Ha Long Bay is a popular place for tourists to visit.

The Vietnamese mouse-deer was thought to have died out more than 30 years ago. Then, scientists found some living in Vietnam in 2019.

Deforestation is also a problem. This is when too many trees are removed from the environment. Deforestation can be caused by logging, fire, and war. The government has been working to replant and keep forests safe.

FACT!

Vietnam is working on building more recycling plants to keep plastic out of its water.

NATIONAL PARKS

Vietnam created its first national park in 1962. Since then, more than 30 other parks have been created.

THE PEOPLE TODAY

Vietnam is a fairly small country, but it has more than 100 million people living in it. Cities are especially crowded. In the 1980s, the Vietnamese government began asking people to move out of cities to make overcrowding less of a problem.

FACT!

Việt kiều, or "Vietnamese overseas," is what Vietnamese people call those who have emigrated, or moved to another country.

Hanoi is so crowded that some people live and work right next to the train tracks.

Most Vietnamese belong to the Viet, or Kinh, ethnic group. These people are related to the country's Native people. However, there are also more than 50 minority ethnic groups. They are collectively called the Degar. The largest Degar group, the Tay, makes up only about 2 percent of the Vietnamese population.

ANGER AT THE GOVERNMENT

When the government asked people to move out of the cities, many of the Degar that live in the countryside were angry. Suddenly, many people were moving in, taking their land, and treating them poorly.

Many people in the Hmong ethnic group are rice farmers in northern Vietnam.

LIFESTYLE

Life in Vietnamese cities is like life in many cities around the world. People have jobs in hospitals, stores, schools, and the government. In their free time, they do things such as read, play video games, and go shopping at night markets.

FACT!
In Vietnam, people wear white instead of black when a loved one dies.

In some parts of Vietnam, people make their living by fishing.

Most Vietnamese today wear Western-style clothing. However, sometimes men and women still wear an outfit called the ao dai.

In the countryside, people spend most of their day farming. Everyone helps, even the elderly and the children.

No matter where they live, Vietnamese people have some things in common. One is a great love for their family. When Vietnamese people make choices, they often think about what's best for the whole family, not just what's best for themselves.

HONORING THE DEAD

Even after death, family is still very important to the Vietnamese. From a young age, children are taught to respect their elders and **ancestors**.

RELIGION

Religion, or faith, is important to many Vietnamese. However, most don't follow an organized religion, or one with a common set of rules. Most Vietnamese citizens practice religion by honoring their ancestors.

Many Vietnamese have a special table called an altar in their house. This is where they put fruit, flowers, and other things to honor their ancestors.

ANIMISM

Many Vietnamese are animistic. This means they believe everything in the world, even nonliving things, has a spirit. Some combine animistic beliefs with the beliefs of an organized religion, such as Buddhism.

About 9 percent of the population is Buddhist. This is the most popular organized religion in Vietnam. Buddhists follow rules called the Eightfold Path, which are meant to help them live a good life. Christianity is also popular thanks to French and American missionaries, or people who spread their faith in other countries. There are small numbers of Hindus, Muslims, and Jews living in the country. They mostly came from other countries.

FACT!

Cao Đài is a religion that started in Vietnam. It combines parts of many different world religions.

Buddhist temples can be found all over Vietnam.

LANGUAGE

The Vietnamese language has been spoken for thousands of years. However, because the Chinese took over so early in the country's history, the language was written using the Chinese writing system for many years. In the 1600s, a new writing system called quốc-ngữ was created. It uses the Latin alphabet, which English also uses.

FACT!

There are more than 80 million people around the world who speak Vietnamese.

People also commonly speak French and English in Vietnam. This school's sign is in both Vietnamese and English.

A few people still write Vietnamese with the Chinese writing system. Today, this is mostly done as a form of art.

The way a word is said in Vietnamese affects its meaning. To make sure this is clear in writing, quốc-ngữ uses many different kinds of marks. For example, *ca* means "sing," but *cá* means "fish."

SHARING THE BIBLE

Quốc-ngữ was created by French and Portuguese missionaries who wanted to spread Christianity in Vietnam. Only the most highly-educated Vietnamese could read Chinese, and the missionaries wanted to make it easier for all people to read the Bible—the holy book of Christianity.

ARTS AND FESTIVALS

People have created music and art in Vietnam since its earliest days. Some of these forms have stayed almost unchanged over the years. For example, people have put on water puppet shows since the 11th century.

FACT!
The dates of many Vietnamese holidays are decided by the lunar, or moon, calendar.

During a water puppet show, puppets are moved around a pool of water. They are controlled by people standing behind a bamboo screen.

Another holiday that honors the dead is called Thanh Minh. On this day, people visit and clean their ancestors' graves. They also bring food and fake money for the dead to use in the afterlife.

The Vietnamese also enjoy many festivals and holidays throughout the year. Some are historical. National Day on September 2 honors the country's independence from France. Reunification Day on April 30 marks the end of the Vietnam War. Other festivals are religious. A Buddhist holiday called Trung Nguyên honors the spirits of the dead. This holiday falls on the 15th day of the 7th lunar month.

TẾT

The most important Vietnamese holiday is Tết, the Vietnamese New Year. It marks the arrival of spring. Families get together to exchange gifts. For good luck in the coming year, they wear red and clean their houses from top to bottom.

FUN AND PLAY

Many Vietnamese enjoy watching and playing sports. Soccer and martial arts are two of the most popular. Kids enjoy playing games such as *Minecraft*, watching TV, and reading comic books. Adults often see shows, play music, and sing and dance together.

FACT!

Vietnam has its own special style of martial arts called Bình Định gia.

Vietnamese adults who live in cities enjoy getting together with friends for drinks and food. They may play chess or a card game called tam cúc.

In the countryside, there are fewer places to go. People may play chess, card games, and musical instruments in the evenings. During Tết, many villages hold rice-cooking contests. Teams race to see who can cook the best rice the fastest. For villages that are near water, these contests often take place on boats.

FOOT BADMINTON

A game called *đá cầu*, or "foot badminton," has been played in Vietnam since the 11th century. It is still popular with adults and children today. In fact, it's considered the country's national sport.

This team of men is taking part in a rice-cooking contest. They must cook the rice without letting the pot touch the ground.

FOOD

Vietnam has many different styles of food. The northern part of the country is very close to the Chinese border, and its most common dishes are very similar to Chinese food. Near the coast, toward the center of the country, most dishes include seafood. In the south, food is more similar to the food of Cambodia and Thailand.

FACT!

Vietnamese coffee is made with condensed milk, which is much thicker and sweeter than regular milk.

The style of Vietnamese food is different depending on where in the country a person is eating.

Throughout the country, pho is a popular dish. This hot soup is made with rice noodles, meat, and spicy broth. Other popular foods include spring rolls and banh mi. This sandwich is commonly made with pork, pickled carrots, cucumber, radish, and fresh cilantro.

FOOD IN HUE

When Vietnam was ruled by kings, they lived in the city of Hue. Even today, the food in Hue is often made to look much prettier than food in other parts of the country—although it's all just as delicious!

Bread wasn't part of the Vietnamese diet until the French took over and brought it with them. After they introduced it, the Vietnamese used it to make the banh mi.

GLOSSARY

ancestor: Someone in your family who lived long before you.

cabinet: The group of people who give advice to the head of a government.

climate: The weather over a long period of time.

Communist: Relating to a system of government in which the central government owns the things that are needed to make and move goods and there is no private property.

constitution: A document that lays out the laws of a country.

delta: The triangular or fan-shaped piece of land made by deposits of mud and sand at the mouth of a river.

economy: The way goods and services are made and sold.

ethnic: Of or relating to large groups of people who have the same cultural background and ways of life.

incense: Material used to produce a pleasing smell when burned.

pandemic: An outbreak of illness that occurs over a wide area and affects many people.

region: A large area of land that has a number of features in common.

resistance: A secret organization fighting against enemy forces.

FIND OUT MORE

Books

Davies, Monika. *Vietnam*. Minneapolis, MN: Bellwether Media, 2023.

Layton, Christine. *Travel to Vietnam*. Minneapolis, MN: Lerner Publications, 2023.

Pham, Thien. *Family Style: Memories of an American from Vietnam*. New York, NY: First Second, 2023.

Websites

Kids World Travel Guide: Vietnam
www.kids-world-travel-guide.com/vietnam-facts.html
Read about Vietnam, and take a look at some cool pictures.

***National Geographic Kids*: Vietnam**
kids.nationalgeographic.com/geography/countries/article/vietnam
Learn more interesting facts about Vietnam.

Video

YouTube: Water Puppet Show, Hanoi
www.youtube.com/watch?v=n8bSD_3xgyA
Watch a short example of water puppetry.

Publisher's note to educators and parents: Our editors have carefully reviewed these websites to ensure that they are suitable for students. Many websites change frequently, however, and we cannot guarantee that a site's future contents will continue to meet our high standards of quality and educational value. Be advised that students should be closely supervised whenever they access the internet.

INDEX

A
agriculture, 4, 5, 6, 12, 17, 19
art, 24

C
caves, 6
China, 5, 8, 12, 22, 23, 28
Chính, Phạm Minh, 11
climate/weather, 4, 6, 7
clothing, 18, 19
Communism, 9, 10
cuisine/food, 27, 28, 29

E
economy, 12, 13
ethnicity, 6, 17
environment, 14, 15

F
festivals, 24, 25
flora/plants, 4, 15
France, 5, 9, 21, 22, 23, 25, 29

G
government, 9, 10, 11, 16, 17

I
immigration, 16

L
Lâm, Tô, 11
language, 22, 23

M
Minh, Ho Chi, 9
mountains, 4, 6, 7

R
religion, 20, 21, 23
rivers, 6, 7

S
sports, 26, 27

T
transportation, 5

U
United States, 12, 21

W
war, 5, 8, 9, 15, 25
wildlife, 15